Drip, drop. Drip, drop. Rain is dripping from the roof of the kennel.

Soon a pool of water is in the middle of the kennel floor.

The pool gets bigger. Soon the dogs are paddling in the water.

They go out into the rain to see Jelly and Bean in the shed.

Oh no! Rain is dripping from the roof of the shed onto the cats' box.

Oh no! The top of the box splits. Now the cats are wet too.

The cats and dogs all go out into the rain to see the pigs in the hut.

Oh no! Rain is dripping from the roof of the hut too!